For you who are made new through the beauty of the Incarnation.

ISBN 978-0-9992773-6-2

www.livetodaywellco.com

Kara Becker and Mary Williams
2018

TABLE OF CONTENTS

When the angels had left them and gone into heaven, the shepherds said to one another, Let us go now to Bethlehem and see this thing that has taken place, which the Lord has ***made known*** *to us. So they went with haste and found Mary and Joseph, and the child lying in the manger. When they saw this, they* ***made known*** *what had been told them about this child.*

Luke 2:15-17

INTRODUCTION

Who were the shepherds that saw the angels? What were they like? Sometimes, we tend to think that miraculous events like this only happen to the greatest among us, but the truth is that the shepherds were average human beings just like you and I. In fact, they were even considered below average socially at the time. And yet, God intentionally chose the shepherds as the first humans to whom He revealed the birth of His son on that first Christmas morning.

When these mud stained, smelly, uneducated individuals heard the angels' message, they immediately went straight to Jesus. They didn't wait to wash themselves or put on clean clothes; why would they? Their hearts were made new by their encounter with the Christ child. Upon realizing the immense magnitude of what they had been told, they shared their joy and amazement with others. The shepherds' hearts and lives were transformed, and their actions showed it.

What are our lives like in the days typically following Christmas? Perhaps you have a few more family gatherings or a New Year's Eve party to attend. Maybe you watch a college football game or engage in friendly debates over how long to leave up the tree. If you're like us, you're probably also deciding on which resolution to ring in January with or taking a few long wintertime naps to recover from the overeating of the season.

But do our actions during those days speak of transformation? Which of our daily activities call to mind the truth revealed to the shepherds and to us? Does the way that we live point towards the glory of God giving us His only Son?

We often hear that we are an Easter people, which is true, but it's also true that we are a people of the Incarnation. The gift of the Incarnation doesn't end on Christmas Day. God presents himself anew to us each and every day. How are WE being made new year-round in light of the truth of Christmas and the joy of the Incarnation?

MADE is an opportunity to rejoice in the greatest Christmas gift we'll ever receive. It's a chance to celebrate the all-year-long transformative power of the Incarnation, and an invitation to delve deeper into the stories of the average women and men in the Bible who have been made new by God's love.

The Israelites, an oppressed people, experienced freedom and the fulfillment of God's promise to them.

Saul, a persecutor whom God struck temporarily blind, became Paul, one of the greatest apostles.

Abraham and Sarah, old in age and barren, conceived through the power of God.

These stories highlight just a few of the many women and men who experienced radical transformation in the hands of God. He desires that same change and freedom for us, if only we allow him to shape and mold us.

Each aspect of MADE was crafted with this goal in mind. Using the Ignatian spiritual practice of imaginative prayer, we rewrote Bible stories using the NRSV edition of the Bible. While the story and direct quotes remain the same, many additional sensory details have been added to help bring the experiences of these women and men to life. We challenge you to enter into their stories with an open heart to see how God might be inviting you more deeply into the joy of the Incarnation.

Perhaps you're using this book during the liturgical Christmas season, the days between the birth of Christ and His baptism, as we praise and reflect on the beauty of the Incarnation.

Maybe you're using this book during the start of the New Year with all of its fresh beginnings, recently made resolutions, and courageous opportunities to embrace positive change and healthy personal growth.

Or perhaps you're using this book during the dawn of a beautiful new season of your life - a new job, relationship, or place to live - and rejoicing in the exciting unfamiliar pieces of your life.

Whether snow is falling against your window and the lights on your Christmas tree still glow in the evening twilight, or it's 95 degrees outside and you're about to dive into the pool, the truths of this season ring true all year long.

Whenever and wherever you find yourself with this book in your hands, know that you are prayed for as you explore how YOU are made new in light of your quiet and reflective ponderings on the Incarnation.

We are

an

Incarnation

people!

HOW TO USE THIS BOOK

WHAT IS IMAGINATIVE PRAYER?

Ignatian Imaginative Prayer is a form of contemplation in which the individual reflects on a specific passage of Scripture using his or her imagination. Throughout this form of prayer, one must draw on the five senses to place his or herself fully within the story by engaging in the sights, smells, noises, and movements of that particular scene.

Ideally, as believers, we do not merely just read or remember the stories of scripture. Instead, we strive to dig deeper into each story so that God can communicate with us in a meaningful and evocative way. Ultimately, the purpose of imaginative prayer is to help us interact and connect with Him on a more intimate and personal level.

HOW DO I USE MADE?

If imaginative prayer sounds confusing or intimidating, don't worry. We worked to ensure that this process will be simple for you! Each passage has already been rewritten using imaginative prayer and we included step by step instructions on each page as well. However, here are a few suggestions to keep in mind:

CLEAR YOUR MIND

At the beginning of each day's reflection, pause. Clear your mind of any worries or anxieties. If your to-do list keeps swirling around your mind, write it down on a piece of paper and then set it to the side. Mentally place yourself in the presence of the Lord.

REFLECT

Read through the entire passage once just to get a sense of the story. Then, read through it again very slowly and mentally place yourself into the scene. Imagine each sensory description in detail, and feel free to add additional details as well. Sometimes it helps to imagine yourself as one of the characters in the scene or as an onlooker. No matter what perspective you choose to pray from, just remain present in the story.

RESPOND

Meditate on the day's reading and ask our Lord what He wishes to reveal to you through this specific passage. We have provided a few questions at the end of each reading to help you respond more fully to the Lord's call.

ONE FINAL, IMPORTANT NOTE

This form of prayer is not about doing. You don't have to journal or talk, though you certainly can do so if you find those methods of prayer helpful. Ultimately, imaginative prayer is all about being present to and with the Lord.

As you start to pray through this book, imaginative prayer may seem totally foreign to you at first. You may find yourself becoming uncomfortable or emotional. That's okay; those emotions are totally normal! Scripture is meant to challenge us and draw us into deeper reflection and meditation.

Acknowledge those feelings and then concentrate on the reading for that day. Breathe in the words of Scripture and visualize the story in your mind and heart.

In these beautiful readings, God introduces us to women and men who have been made new through the power of the Incarnation. Now, it is our turn to allow the birth of Christ to transform every aspect of our lives and our hearts. Come and rest in Him.

ABOUT THE ART

The Maker intentionally draws His brush across the empty canvas as He creates His finest art.

We are always in a constant act of being made new. As long as we remain open to God's unending grace, we will continually be transformed. We are never finished.

The brush moves and flips across the piece. Bits of paint stick here. Globs of paint move over there. Every movement is filled with His loving purpose.

The twists and turns of the brushstrokes on these pages mirror the brush strokes of our lives. The simple movements mimic those moments in which we are caught in joyful surprise or learn challenging lessons. Each day presents new opportunities to let go of the lies that hold us back and step out in courage and faith. The more that we lean into these opportunities, the more fully we become our true selves.

The Artist gazes at the beauty of his masterpiece. Its completeness is known only to Him.

Because we are human, our self understanding might be in bits and pieces, but the fullness of who we are shall one day be revealed when we meet our Maker. We may feel ordinary, simple, and unworthy, much like the shepherds felt on that first Christmas night. But the truth remains - we are His beloved, His greatest creation.

We pray that the simple brush strokes throughout MADE remind you that you are created with deep purpose and love by God. Our hope is that you allow Him to continually transform you and that you may experience the joy of being made new by His love.

DAY ONE

The Shepherds' Encounter with the Lord
Luke 2:15-20

In today's reading, we encounter the shepherds. God handpicked these ordinary human beings to be the first witnesses to the Incarnation. Upon meeting the infant Jesus, they were transformed and rushed out to make known the good news to the rest of the world.

Before you read, pause and clear your mind. Center yourself in God's presence and read through the scripture once. Then, choose a perspective to enter into the scene. Are you one of the characters or a silent observer? Regardless, know that this moment is full of grace.
Allow Him to make you new.

Dazed, the men stared at the night sky. The once blinding light that had radiated from the angels now faded, leaving behind only the twinkling dots of the stars above. One of the shepherds leaned against a nearby tree, allowing its weather-beaten bark to support his weight, while another man lay still on the ground, too dumbfounded to rise to his feet.

The eldest among them combed his fingers through his scratchy beard and leaned on his wooden staff. After a few moments of silence, he pointed a crooked finger towards the shadowy outline of a city in the distance. He urged the other shepherds to action, saying, "Let us go now to Bethlehem and see this thing that has taken place, which the Lord has made known to us."

Stumbling to their feet, the men began to plod in a dream-like fashion down the hill, for they were not fully recovered from the shock of the angels' appearance. Before long, however, their pace quickened as they raced forward through the gently waving grass.

Soon, the shepherds arrived at a humble barn. A bright star stood guard over the sloped straw roof, lighting the way inside. After a moment of hesitation, the eldest shepherd stepped forward, his fingers brushing against the wooden door as he swung it open. One by one, the other shepherds followed him inside.

Within the barn, their eyes fell upon the figure of a woman, clothed in a simple woven dress, kneeling next to a makeshift cradle. Her attention was wholly devoted to the small infant, who softly wailed inside the cradle. As she tended to the babe, a man stepped forward from the shadows. He approached the shepherds slowly with his staff in his hand and questions brewing in his eyes.

The shepherds, now crowded around the corners of the tiny barn, fell to their knees. Tears sprang to their eyes as they began to describe in breathless voices what had been made known to them about this child. As they spoke of the appearance of the angels and their astounding words, Mary and Joseph listened with amazement.

When they finished their tale, Joseph clapped the shepherds on their shoulders and conversed in hushed tones with them, while Mary turned away from the men and back towards the unassuming babe who lay among the pile of straw. She began to stroke his face tenderly and quietly pondered the shepherds' words in her heart.

After a short while, the shepherds left the barn and headed back towards their fields. Though they initially just whispered excitedly to one another, before long, they were whooping with glee, shouting the good news at the top of their lungs as they made their way through the darkened city streets. A shocked housewife gasped as a shepherd grabbed her by the shoulders and shared the good news. After shaking off his grasp and dismissing him curtly, she hurried inside, eager to be away from the apparent madman before her. Undeterred, the shepherd continued glorifying and praising God for all that he had heard and seen.

HOW ARE YOU MADE NEW?

When you ponder the glory of the Incarnation,
what thoughts first spring to mind?

How can you live out the same joy that the shepherds
had through your interactions with others?

What part of this story most resonated with you?
How does it apply to your own life?

Let us go now
to Bethlehem
and see this thing
that has taken place,
which the Lord
has made known to us.
Luke 2:15

DAY TWO

The Creation of the World
Genesis 1:1-31

In the beginning, there was only God. Then, our loving Creator molded and shaped each aspect of the world, including us. The story of who we are and the root of our identity rests in Love.

Before you read, pause and clear your mind. Center yourself in God's presence and read through the scripture once. Then, choose a perspective to enter into the scene. Are you one of the characters or a silent observer? Regardless, know that this moment is full of grace.
Allow Him to make you new.

God was.

And then, a command. "Let there be light." Suddenly, a wind swept over the waters, and brilliant rays exploded above the formless horizon, sparkling, dancing, and rejoicing. Light.

At the exhalation of His breath, swiftly swirling, the waters separated, creating a vast dome that was vibrant and clear and boundless. Sky.

Then the waters pulled together, as if He was inhaling the wetness. Powerful waves crashed upon each other over and over, the intensity rapidly building. This process continued until finally, the waves smashed so forcefully together that a cracking noise became audible, and dry earth rose up from the depths. Land.

"Let the earth put forth vegetation," He joyfully cried. Slowly and gently at first, seedlings started to sprout, pressing up from the land and dotting the landscape. Then the seedlings grew more quickly, spreading wildly with no end in sight. Stems, leaves, trees, flowers, and fruit began budding, blooming, and blossoming, each in their turn, until vegetation flourished all over the land.

Then the Lord commanded, "Let there be lights in the dome of the sky to separate the day from the night." As darkness fell and the fiery, warm light sank below the lush, green, textured horizon, an awe-inspiring dance began. Millions upon millions of twinkling lights lit up the sky, with each glimmering star individually placed so as to draw the eyes up and up toward Love himself. Suddenly, all at once, a larger, white light illuminated the sky. It sparkled brightly and then became cooler and calmer, radiating hope in the shallow darkness of night.

Stillness abruptly vanished as the creator God designed all living creatures. A flash of uninhibited movement across the sky was followed by an exuberant roar from beyond the trees and, from beneath the blue waters, a nimble maneuver. A great trembling rumbled in the earth as wild creatures bolted across the land, sea, and sky. The commotion increased as each one began joyfully leaping, flying, creeping, and swimming. Each breathed in their freedom.

And yet, in the midst of all this tremendous beauty and goodness, there was more to be done.

God said, "Let us make humankind in our image, according to our likeness; and let them have dominion over the fish of the sea, and over the birds of the air, and over the cattle, and over all the wild animals of the earth, and over every creeping thing that creeps upon the earth."

And it was so. Unfurling fingers, extending toes... the back stretching to full height as hair spilled over its shoulders. Before long, eyes opened, ears listened, and senses felt on fire. The first exquisite inhale of Love's most intimate creation.

Male first. Then female. Given life. Given hope. Given love by Love.

And it was all good. Very good.

HOW ARE YOU MADE NEW?

Which imagery from the Creation story most speaks to you? Why?

As you consider our world's beginnings, what feelings surface in your heart?

How does the knowledge that you have been made by Love affect how you will choose to live your life going forward?

Let us make
humankind in our image,
according to our likeness.
Genesis 1:26

DAY THREE

The Discovery of the Empty Tomb
John 20:1-8

Mary Magdalene's world is rocked when she discovers the empty tomb on that first Easter morning. Through Jesus' dying and rising, humanity was changed forever. Through Him, we are given the hope of experiencing new life.

Before you read, pause and clear your mind. Center yourself in God's presence and read through the scripture once. Then, choose a perspective to enter into the scene. Are you one of the characters or a silent observer? Regardless, know that this moment is full of grace.
Allow Him to make you new.

As the darkness of night faded and the Sabbath day drew to a close, Mary Magdalene plodded wearily through the garden. On her arm she carried a wicker basket which was full of burial spices. The fragrant aromas of the spices wafted upward, reminding her of what had transpired less than two days before. Her tear stained eyes scanned the garden in search of several men to help her roll away the stone.

Suddenly, she gasped in astonishment and her eyes widened. Though the tomb remained in place, the massive, towering stone which had blocked the entrance was cast to the side. A wave of emotion washed over her, filling her with sensations of amazement, terror, and fury. Had Jesus' body been stolen? Had Pilate ordered his body moved? How could this stone, which required the strenuous effort of several men to move, have been displaced without any clearly visible explanation?

Anger filled Mary Magdalene and she clenched her fists tightly. Whirling around, she began to sprint back through the garden. As she ran along the path, her feet stumbled over tree roots and jagged rocks. The brambles pulling at her dress did not slow her pace as she darted round the corner and past a grove of olive trees. A cool breeze whipped through her hair until she finally arrived, breathless, at the doorstep of a modest house.

Impatiently, she flew up the stairs and threw open a wooden door, startling the occupants inside. A group of men were seated around the room, muttering in hushed tones, but all fell silent at the sight of the frantic woman before them.

Still gasping for air, she grasped the arm of Simon Peter who stood near the doorway. Concern filled his eyes, but she brushed him aside as he leaned forward to calm her. Gesturing wildly towards the road, she stammered, "They have taken the Lord out of the tomb, and we do not know where they have laid him!"

Peter and the other disciple, the one whom Jesus loved, immediately sprang to their feet. Leaving behind their woven cloaks in their haste, they rushed out of the house. Dust clouds rose behind them as their feet pounded down the dirt road and then through the garden. Soon Peter fell behind and the other disciple outran him, arriving at the tomb first. Bending down, he peered into the shadows of the tomb. Before him lay the linen wrappings on the stone floor, but no body. He hesitated at the entrance, confusion filling his eyes. Rubbing his sweaty palms together, he leaned against the entrance of the tomb to ponder what he had seen.

After a few moments, Simon Peter, trembling and out of breath, arrived and rushed into the tomb. His once sure steps screeched to a halt as he discovered the linen cloth, which had been wrapped around Jesus' head, rolled up and set to the side. The remaining linen wrappings, which were clearly empty, lay strewn across the room. Astonished, he braced himself against the wall, hoarsely calling to the other disciple to join him. As the other disciple went into the tomb, hopeful tears filled his eyes, and he saw and believed.

HOW ARE YOU MADE NEW?

Have you had an experience of great surprise? What happened?

In the ordinary moments of your life, how does His resurrection make you new?

Does your hope in Him help develop who you are? If so, how?

He saw and believed.

John 20:8

DAY FOUR

God's Appearance to Abraham
Genesis 17:1-5,15-17,22

In today's reading, God forges a covenant with Abraham and promises that Abraham's wife, Sarah, will bear a son. Despite their disbelief, God fulfills His promise. Abraham and Sarah are made new, though the fruits of God's covenant are not fully revealed to them until later.

Before you read, pause and clear your mind. Center yourself in God's presence and read through the scripture once. Then, choose a perspective to enter into the scene. Are you one of the characters or a silent observer? Regardless, know that this moment is full of grace. Allow Him to make you new.

Coughing heavily, Abram wiped his mouth on his elbow and paused by the side of the road. Though the sun was not yet blazing high above, already his back ached from the work of the day. Now ninety-nine years in age, he longed for the days when his body worked as he commanded it to. Sighing heavily, he leaned on his wooden staff and continued plodding down the dusty covered street slowly, one foot dragging slightly behind him.

Suddenly, the twinkling of the stars in the near-dawn sky vanished entirely. A brilliant, white light burst out of nothing, causing Abram to cry out and stumble. Stooping low to the ground, he shielded his eyes with one palm in an unsuccessful effort to clear his vision. A booming voice echoed through the valley, "I am God Almighty; walk before me, and be blameless. And I will make my covenant between me and you, and will make you exceedingly numerous."

Stunned, Abram froze momentarily before crashing to ground and prostrating himself before the Lord. Terror and awe rocked his aged body as the voice renamed him, saying, "No longer shall your name be Abram but your name shall be Abraham, for I have made you the ancestor of a multitude of nations." Abraham, wetting his lips, tried to stammer a reply, but found his mouth dry and tongue silent.

God continued and told Abraham that from then on Abraham's wife, Sarai, would be known as Sarah. Rising slightly to his knees, Abraham kept his forehead bowed low to the ground as he listened intently, but the next words he heard so filled him with emotion that he started sputtering.

"I will bless her, and moreover I will give you a son by her. I will bless her, and she shall give rise to nations; kings of peoples shall come from her," bellowed the voice.

At these words, all that Abraham could do was laugh until his belly ached. He fell forward into the dust, howling and clutching his tunic to his chest. Tears of humor dropped from his eyes as he managed to gasp between chuckles, "Can a child be born to a man who is a hundred years old?" Still cackling, Abraham muttered to himself, "Can Sarah, who is ninety years old, bear a child?" Shaking his head back and forth, he stared at the white light above him.

Then God reassured Abraham and explained to him the covenant he intended to establish with Abraham and Abraham's descendants. And when He had finished talking with him, God went up from Abraham.

HOW ARE YOU MADE NEW?

Have you ever been changed by an experience or person and didn't realize it until much later? What happened?

Can you relate to Abraham's disbelief in the story, and if so, in what area of your life? How can you lean further into God's love to conquer that disbelief?

What covenant do you feel the Lord asking you to make with Him?

Walk before me,
and be blameless.
Genesis 17:1

DAY FIVE

The Presentation of Jesus
Luke 2:25-35

For many years, Simeon waited patiently in the knowledge that God would reveal the Messiah to him before his death. In today's reading, Simeon finally meets Jesus, the source of his salvation.

Before you read, pause and clear your mind. Center yourself in God's presence and read through the scripture once. Then, choose a perspective to enter into the scene. Are you one of the characters or a silent observer? Regardless, know that this moment is full of grace.
Allow Him to make you new.

Now there was a righteous and devout man in Jerusalem whose name was Simeon. Though his posture was stooped and his age advanced, the gentleness in his eyes and the wisdom in his words earned the respect of all the Jews. Many years before, the Holy Spirit had revealed to Simeon that he would not die before he had seen the Lord's Messiah.

One morning, as the sun rose and began to paint the sky in a swath of vivid colors, Simeon was where he could usually be found – within the high walls of the temple. Kneeling before the altar, he bowed his forehead and pressed it lightly against the cool stone floor.

After a while, Simeon sank back on his heels to rub his aching back. Sensing that he was not alone, he glanced up just in time to see two figures entering through the doorway to the temple. The golden hues of the sun streamed in behind them, temporarily blinding Simeon until the couple stepped forward. Squinting, he stood up and prepared to greet them.

As the couple approached, it was apparent that though purple and brown shadows encircled the couples' eyes, joy radiated from their faces. The woman smiled quietly at Simeon, her brown eyes dancing, as her husband leaned forward to firmly shake Simeon's hand. Within the woman's arms lay a tiny infant, protectively swaddled in linen. The babe wailed softly, prompting the mother to caress his face and whisper reassuringly into his ear.

Nodding at the couple, Simeon rolled back the sleeves of his tunic. It was clear to him that, following the Jewish custom, the couple had come to offer their son to God and request purification.

Tenderly, he lifted the infant from his mother's arms. As he cradled the babe, Simeon suddenly drew a sharp breath. Shakily, he lifted a finger and touched the child's forehead. Almost immediately, he jerked his hand back as if it was on fire. His once pale cheeks flushed, and his wrinkled face slowly spread into an incredulous smile.

Gazing upward, Simeon began to praise God, saying, "Master, now you are dismissing your servant in peace, according to your word; for my eyes have seen your salvation, which you have prepared in the presence of all peoples, a light for revelation to the Gentiles, and for glory to your people Israel."

Astonished, the child's father, Joseph, gripped his wife's hand tightly, pondering over the meaning of Simeon's words. After a few moments, Simeon seemed to rise from his reverie, and he turned towards Mary and Joseph. Lifting a hand, he blessed them.

Then, as he slipped the baby back from his own arms into those of the child's mother, he remarked to Mary, "This child is destined for the falling and the rising of many in Israel, and to be a sign that will be opposed so that the inner thoughts of many will be revealed—and a sword will pierce your own soul too."

HOW ARE YOU MADE NEW?

Have you ever had to wait patiently for an answer to your prayers? What happened and how did God respond?

What is it about the act of waiting that transforms the human heart? How has waiting transformed yours?

Simeon saw God's salvation through Jesus's presence in this story. How do you experience God's salvation anew each and every day?

My eyes have seen your salvation.

Luke 2:30

DAY SIX

The Finding of Jesus in the Temple
Luke 2:41-52

Though Mary and Joseph knew that their son was special, they could not fully comprehend the depths of what God had in store for Jesus. In this reading, Mary and Joseph search frantically for their child. Their understanding of God's will and plan is made new when they find Jesus in the temple.

Before you read, pause and clear your mind. Center yourself in God's presence and read through the scripture once. Then, choose a perspective to enter into the scene. Are you one of the characters or a silent observer? Regardless, know that this moment is full of grace. Allow Him to make you new.

When the great festival of Passover drew to a close, the families chattered happily with one another as they loaded up their great wagons. The caravan moved slowly as it left Jerusalem, for the wagons were mightily weighed down and the crowd of people made it difficult to proceed quickly. Some of the younger children sprinted back and forth between wagons whooping loudly, while the teenagers lounged in the back of the wagons, playing games together. The mothers were content to let their children roam free. Together, the women reflected on the highlights of the feast with their dearest friends as they broke bread together.

When the darkness of night shrouded the sky and the wee babes began rubbing their eyes, the caravan prepared to stop and rest. It was then that Mary first began to look for Jesus, for her twelve year old son was nowhere to be seen. As she wandered from one glowing fire to another in search of her son, she laughed and joked with her friends and family. Surely Jesus was over there… or perhaps over there.

Before long though, the families began to turn in for the night, tucking their children safely beneath warm blankets. Her anxiety growing, Mary enlisted Joseph's help and together they searched for Jesus, but no one had seen their son. Though fear turned and twisted her stomach, Mary wrapped her cloak around her shoulders and hardened her resolve.

As night turned to day, it was clear that no one in the caravan knew where Jesus was. By this point, both parents were frantic to find their son, and so they returned in haste to Jerusalem.

On the third day after Jesus' disappearance, as they wandered through the busy city streets, steady tears flowed down Mary's cheeks, stinging her lips. Hand in hand, Mary and Joseph stumbled wearily up the stone steps to the temple. Despite the fear tugging on their hearts, they knew they needed to enter the temple – after all, this was where they had last seen their son.

As they entered the temple and genuflected, a strange sight confronted them. The normally vast temple was filled with people so dense in number that it grew difficult to walk. Mary elbowed her way gently to the middle of the crowd, past elder after elder, until she saw at last the source of the commotion. Here she found her young son, a mere boy of twelve, seated in the center of the wisest elders, with his palms resting on his cheeks. He sat calmly amongst the chattering group, listening intently, asking them questions, and offering answers to their commentary. Everyone who heard Jesus' words ring out over the din were amazed at the depth of his understanding and wisdom.

Astonished, Mary drew Jesus close to her side and after hugging him, reproachfully said, "Child, why have you treated us like this? Look, your father and I have been searching for you in great anxiety." Jesus gazed serenely upon his mother's anxious face and replied, "Why were you searching for me? Did you not know that I must be in my Father's house?"

Mary and Joseph were so shocked by his words that they did not reprimand him, but instead, they hesitated for a moment. Confusion washed over their faces, for they did not not yet understand the meaning of his words. Then Mary beckoned to Jesus, and he obediently left with his parents to return to Nazareth. As Jesus grew older and wiser, His mother treasured all of these things in her heart.

HOW ARE YOU MADE NEW?

Who do you most relate to in this story? Why?

Recall the experience of losing something precious to you.
What happened? How did the experience change you?

Are you able to name a time when you felt lost in life?
How did God guide you through that experience?

The elders listened to Jesus and marveled at his wisdom and understanding.
How can you let Christ teach you that true wisdom?

His mother treasured all these
things in her heart.
Luke 2:51

The Entrance into the Promised Land
Joshua 1:1-9,3

For forty years, the Israelites wandered the desert in search of the Promised Land. In today's reading, they finally cross the Jordan River. The transformation of the Israelites' hearts was not the result of reaching their goal, but instead one of enduring patience and fortitude during their long wait.

Before you read, pause and clear your mind. Center yourself in God's presence and read through the scripture once. Then, choose a perspective to enter into the scene. Are you one of the characters or a silent observer? Regardless, know that this moment is full of grace. Allow Him to make you new.

The words that the Lord had spoken to Joshua just days before were whispered from soul to soul around the camp. "I hereby command you: Be strong and courageous; do not be frightened or dismayed, for the Lord your God is with you wherever you go."

As the families gathered together and cooked breakfast around their campfires they pondered the meaning of these words. *Be strong? Be courageous? What more must we endure? For forty years, we have been wandering. We are lost. Lord, when will you deliver us to your promised land?*

Shortly after breakfast came the command to gather their belongings and collect their livestock. The few wares and goods that each family called their own were bundled up in canvas and tied together with thick rope. Wagons were hastily packed as they all prepared to leave. A new journey was to begin.

Gradually, a large crowd assembled on the shore of the Jordan River. The clamorous sounds of conversation filled the hot desert air. A mixture of fatigue, excitement, reluctancy, and worry buzzed among them as they waited for the next instruction. Several vultures cawed and circled noisily overhead as the heat of the morning sun bore down upon their heads, causing them to drip with sweat.

A wave of silence fell over the crowd as they watched a group of men bend low, staggering under the weight of the Ark of the Covenant. Slowly, they carried the Holy of Holies to the edge of the water. Suddenly, the wind began to pick up, swirling the woven cloaks around their bodies. Clouds of dust and sand flew into their faces, and they attempted to shield their eyes.

With a loud, roaring sound, the murky river water appeared to be growing taller and taller, until it towered far above their heads. All at once, the Jordan separated into two. Dry land now replaced what had been covered by swift currents just moments earlier. The whole crowd froze in place, shock and disbelief coursing through their bodies. Some of the elders nodded solemnly in reverence as only they remembered their narrow escape from Pharaoh across the Red Sea so many years ago.

Then, arriving just as quickly, silence and stillness permeated the scene. The howling winds ceased and the whirling dust fell to the feet of the people. From ahead came the command to continue their walk. As the crowd picked their way across the dry river bed, awe and wonder filled their hearts. The Spirit of the Lord was upon them.

Toward the end of the large caravan, a small boy inched closer to the edge of the river waiting for his turn to cross. As he approached the Jordan, the child looked up at his mother with deep fear in his eyes, Will the water come crashing down on us? I don't know how to swim! I'm afraid! His mother looked at him reassuringly and in hushed tones murmured, "My son, be strong and courageous."

Resolutely putting one foot in front of the other while still clutching his mother's fingers tightly in this own, he finally reached the other side of the river. After breathing a sigh of relief, he surveyed the view before him. Awestruck, he observed something he had only been told in stories - the Promised Land.

HOW ARE YOU MADE NEW?

Has the choice to be strong and courageous played a part of your spiritual life?
How were you changed through that choice?

When have you experienced God's transformative love
because of a time of endurance in your life?

As God had a plan for the Israelites, so, too, He has a plan for you.
Have you doubted in God's plans for your future?
How do you combat that fear?

Be strong and courageous.

Joshua 1:6

DAY EIGHT

The Annunciation
Luke 1:26-31,34-38

When Mary learns that she will soon become the mother of Jesus,
the angel reassures her that nothing will be impossible for God.
Through her fiat, her yes, she allows God to mold and shape her life.

Before you read, pause and clear your mind. Center yourself in God's presence and read through the scripture once. Then, choose a perspective to enter into the scene. Are you one of the characters or a silent observer? Regardless, know that this moment is full of grace.
Allow Him to make you new.

Mary sighed contentedly, pausing for a moment to rest her tired fingers. As she patted the damp dough between her hands, she gazed out the window. In the yard, chickens were noisily clucking and pecking at the ground as her father scattered grain for them to eat.

Turning around, Mary wiped her hands on a rag and prepared to slip the bread into the fire to be cooked. Suddenly, her eyes widened and her jaw dropped. Behind her, near the stone fireplace, a different kind of light appeared. Rather than the warm flickering tones of the blazing fire built within the hearth, Mary saw a soft, glowing light slowly expand. As it grew in intensity and size, she spotted a brilliant figure within the light. Beckoning to her, it said, "Greetings, favored one! The Lord is with you."

Surprised and perplexed, Mary trembled, knelt on the ground, and bowed her head low, pondering what sort of greeting this might be. The angel's tinkling voice sounded again, as it reassured, "Do not be afraid, Mary, for you have found favor with God. And now, you will conceive in your womb and bear a son, and you will name him Jesus."

As the angel continued to explain how great her son would be and how He would reign over a kingdom without end, Mary felt her confusion growing. Nervously, she wrung her hands as she silently listened to all that the angel had to say. After a few moments, with anxiety building in her heart, Mary timidly inquired, "How can this be, since I am a virgin?"

Smiling gently, the angel said, "The Holy Spirit will come upon you, and the power of the Most High will overshadow you; therefore the child to be born will be holy; He will be called Son of God." And then, to calm and encourage Mary, the angel added, "And now, your relative Elizabeth in her old age has also conceived a son; and this is the sixth month for her who was said to be barren. For nothing will be impossible with God."

Then Mary tucked her long hair behind one ear, folded her hands in her lap, and humbly replied, "Here am I, the servant of the Lord; let it be with me according to your word." With tears in her eyes, she watched as the angel departed from her.

HOW ARE YOU MADE NEW?

How does this reading change your understanding of what it means to say "yes" to God, and how can that apply to your life?

Do you truly believe nothing is impossible for God? Why or why not?

Ponder an experience in which you had to make a difficult decision. How did your faith in God play a part of that moment?

Let it be with me
according to your word.
Luke 1:38

DAY NINE

The Conversion of Saul
Acts 9:1-8

In a single moment, Saul's world turned upside down. When he lost his eyesight, he also lost sight of all he had ever known and came face to face with Truth. In spite of his sinfulness, God offered him redemption and a chance to be made new in Christ.

Before you read, pause and clear your mind. Center yourself in God's presence and read through the scripture once. Then, choose a perspective to enter into the scene. Are you one of the characters or a silent observer? Regardless, know that this moment is full of grace.
Allow Him to make you new.

Still cursing under his breath, Saul hurried down the busy road, his feet kicking up clouds of dirt behind him. Layers of grime coated his woven tunic, and the oppressive heat of the afternoon sun beat down upon him as he rushed towards Damascus.

Saul had just left the high priest in Jerusalem. Within the heavy leather pack on his back lay letters from the high priest. These letters were intended to help Saul enter the synagogues in Damascus and seek out Christians.

Saul could not help grinning a little as he envisioned his triumphant return to Jerusalem after his journey. He could see it now… In his vision, Saul pictured himself jubilantly entering the city, followed by the Christians who had caused so much trouble and confusion. Saul's eyes narrowed as he thought of the gullible men and women who needed to be brought forward to face justice.

Now, with the letters in hand, Saul made his way towards Damascus with several friends to aid him in his endeavor. While his companions joked with one another, Saul lifted one hand to slap a fly that buzzed irritatingly around his neck. The men bantered back and forth as they continued on their journey.

Suddenly, a light from heaven flashed before his eyes. As he dived to the ground, Saul cried out in shock and fear. The dazzling, white light spread rapidly until it consumed his vision entirely. In an instant, his once clear and able eyes saw nothing but a pitch black empty void.

Reeling in pain, Saul clenched his fists as a deep booming voice echoed forth in the darkness, vibrating in the depths of Saul's soul. "Saul," cried the voice. "Saul, why do you persecute me?" Terrified, Saul's voice quivered as he responded, "Who are you, Lord?"

After an agonizing moment of silence for Saul, the reply came, "I am Jesus, whom you are persecuting." Confusion and fear coursed through Saul's body as the voice added, "But get up and enter the city, and you will be told what you are to do."

The men who were traveling with Saul stood speechless, for though they had heard the voice, they could see no one. Terrified to move, they remained rooted in their spots. As the voice departed, Saul rolled over onto his stomach in the dirt. Panting a little, he pushed himself onto his knees.

Despite the fact that his eyes were open, Saul still saw nothing. Shaking nervously from his encounter with the Lord, he began to grasp around wildly for his pack and staff. After finding neither and realizing that he was unable to stand up on his own, he called out. After a moment of hesitation, his friends stepped forward to help him, anxiously peering over their shoulders to make sure that they, too, would not be struck blind. Together, his companions lifted him by the arms, and supporting his weight between them, started carrying him down the road leading to Damascus.

HOW ARE YOU MADE NEW?

When have you been blind to or ignored what the Lord wanted of you?

Have you ever felt the Lord transforming you in a single moment? What happened?

Have you ever pictured a triumph over others like Saul envisioned in the beginning of the story? How can you conquer that temptation with humility?

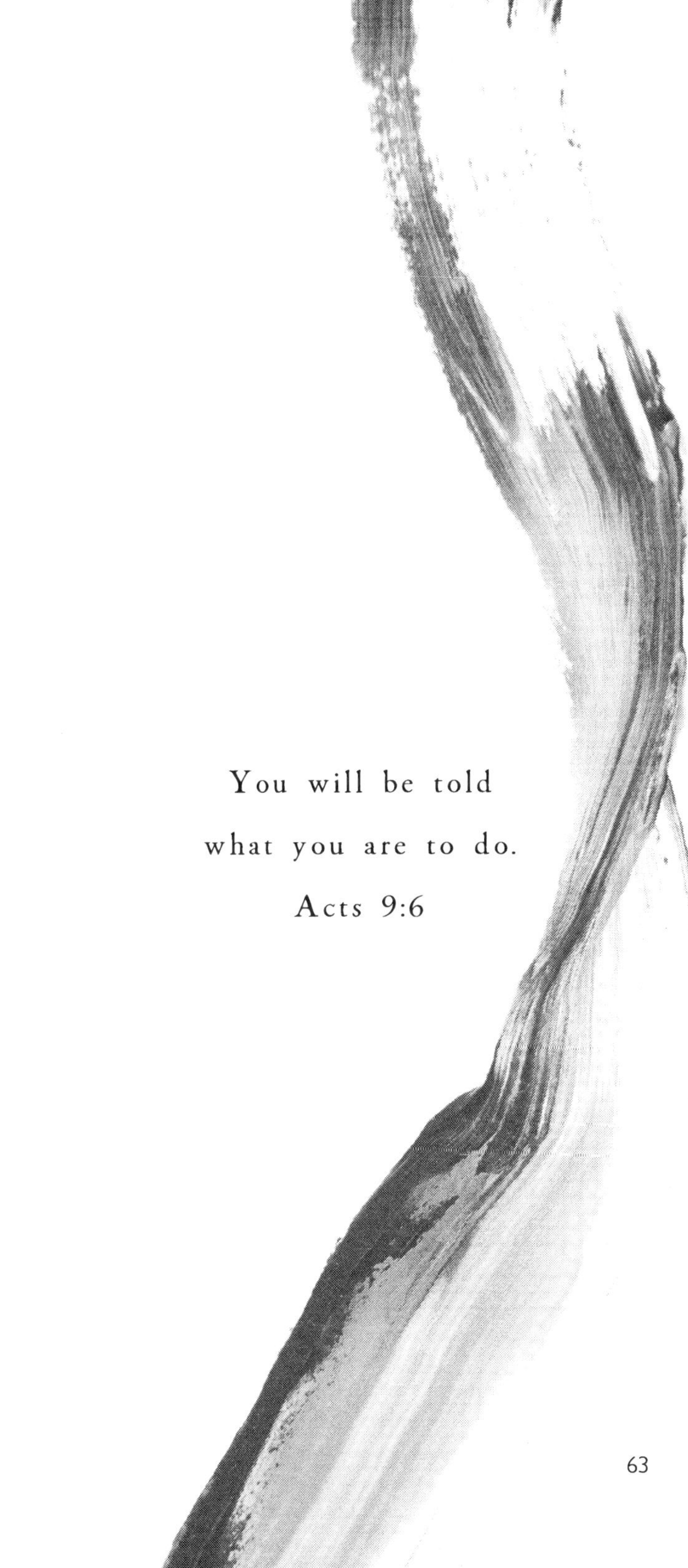

You will be told
what you are to do.
Acts 9:6

DAY TEN

Jesus's Call to the Disciples
Matthew 4:18-20

In today's reading, we experience Peter's and Andrew's shock upon receiving the invitation of a lifetime. When they freely choose to follow Jesus, He remakes them by tearing down the lies that they believed about their identity and purpose in life.

Before you read, pause and clear your mind. Center yourself in God's presence and read through the scripture once. Then, choose a perspective to enter into the scene. Are you one of the characters or a silent observer? Regardless, know that this moment is full of grace.
Allow Him to make you new.

Jesus gazed out over the glistening sea. As He ran His fingers through His wind-blown hair, the warmth of the afternoon sun dancing on His cheeks brought a smile to His face. He closed His eyes for a moment and silently uttered a prayer of gratitude to His Father.

Upon finishing His prayer, Jesus' gaze scanned the shore. Several small boats were moored securely to a weathered dock, and they bobbed gently up and down on the waves. In the water a few women were scrubbing clothes with rocks while their children joyfully splashed each other alongside them. A little further down the beach, two men were preparing to cast a large net into the sea. Their heads were bent as their sturdy fingers labored to untangle the coarse rope of the net. Seeing their determination at the task at hand, Jesus chuckled to himself and walked towards them, His toes dipping into the edge of the water as He walked.

Soon He stood beside the men. Calmly, He issued the invitation, "Follow me."

Their attention entirely consumed by their work, Peter and Andrew had not heard Jesus' footsteps padding softly along the beach as He approached. Startled by the sound of His voice, Peter jumped a little and then glanced at Andrew. Peter's eyes showed confusion as he wondered who on earth this man was and what he was talking about. The man was unknown to him, yet He also seemed strangely familiar. Andrew, too, had now stood up and was staring at the man with fascination.

Neither man could explain why, but they were drawn to Him. Something about Him seemed radiant, and it wasn't just the sun glittering through the willowy trees behind Him. Unable to draw their eyes away, the two men stared as Jesus grinned, His face gentle yet confident.

Beckoning to them, He said, "Follow me, and I will make you fish for people." With arms wide open, He pointed down the beach and towards the town, which was nestled among rolling green hills.

Something about His words struck their hearts. Without pause, Peter and Andrew let the nets drop from their hands into the soft, wet sand. Then, stepping out of the water, they began to amble slowly alongside Jesus on the shore. Curiously, they gazed at Him, their hearts filled with awe.

HOW ARE YOU MADE NEW?

How and why have you been drawn to the Lord and chosen following Him?

What are some practical steps you can take to put God first in your life?

What do you believe to be your purpose in life?
How would you describe your identity in Christ?

Follow me.

Matthew 4:19

DAY ELEVEN

The Epiphany
Matthew 2:1-2,9-12

When the wise men chose to drop everything and follow the star, many people likely thought they were crazy. And yet, the wise men did not hesitate to go where God was calling them. As they adored the Christ child and offered Him their finest gifts, they realized that they had received the greatest gift of all.

Before you read, pause and clear your mind. Center yourself in God's presence and read through the scripture once. Then, choose a perspective to enter into the scene. Are you one of the characters or a silent observer? Regardless, know that this moment is full of grace.
Allow Him to make you new.

In the time of King Herod, after Jesus was born in Bethlehem, wise men from the East came to Jerusalem. Draped in colorful silk robes and seated upon heavily laden camels, the wise men entered the city and began to inquire, "Where is the child who has been born King of the Jews? For we observed his star at its rising, and have come to pay him homage." From tavern to tavern and marketplace to marketplace they traveled, asking all whom they encountered.

It was a crisp, cool night in Bethlehem when they set out again. Having finished their conversation with Herod, the wise men departed once more in search of the source of the star. Pulling their thick fur cloaks closer to their skin, the wise men shivered a little as they led their camels down one city street after another. The tinkling of the bells on their camels' harnesses was the only sound to be heard, for everyone else was tucked comfortably inside their homes, safe and warm.

One of the wise men lifted his hands to his mouth and blew on them gently before rubbing them together. As he peered into the lighted windows of the houses nearby, he observed families gathered around their tables, breaking bread and laughing with one another.

Suddenly, a twinkling, brilliant light far above them caught his attention. Inhaling a deep breath, he called out to his fellow wise men and spurred his camel on with his attention fixated on the star above. It was the same star they had seen at its rising, and the wise men fell into a single line as they guided their camels in that direction.

After what felt like hours, the star halted over a humble barn. Overwhelmed with joy, the wise men quickly dismounted their camels. Impatiently, they tossed the edges of their cloaks back over their shoulders and strode towards the barn. Hearing the commotion, a man stepped out through the entrance to meet them. After bowing low before them, he introduced himself as the carpenter, Joseph. The wise men responded to his greeting, and after a short conversation, Joseph led them into the barn.

Upon stepping over the threshold, the wise men let out a collective gasp at the sight before their eyes. Great gaping holes dotted the straw roof, spilling moonlight within and illuminating each corner of the barn. The smell of manure wafted through the air, and a pig snorted softly at them. Mice scurried back and forth over the creaking floor boards, and a cat, perched lazily in the rafters, eyed the wise men suspiciously. But the wise men barely spared a glance for any of these things.

Instead, their attention was wholly consumed with a small infant who lay within his mother's loving arms. Mary, his mother, patted the baby's back, and after he let out a tiny burp, she began to cradle him in her arms. Shyly, she turned him so that the wise men could see his face.

As they gazed upon the babe, the wise men bowed their heads and bent their knees, which scraped softly against the floor. Then the wise men began to sing beautiful hymns of praise to God, their deep voices creating a rich harmony. Tears of gratitude and awe sprung to their eyes, and their hearts were glad.

After a few moments, one of the wise men stood up and went outside to the camels. He returned shortly, pulling behind him a small cart full of ornately carved chests. One by one, the wise men opened these richly decorated treasured chests and drew forth gifts of shimmering gold, frankincense, and myrrh. These were each presented to the babe in turn, causing Mary to gasp in astonishment and Joseph to involuntarily tighten his grasp on Mary's shoulder.

Finally, their worship finished and packages delivered, the wise men prepared to leave. Having been warned in a dream not to return to Herod, they regretfully left for their own county by another road, pondering the gift they had just received.

HOW ARE YOU MADE NEW?

Have you ever been changed through the experience of giving someone else a gift?
What happened?

What physical or spiritual gift has most changed your life? How so?

God guided the wise men silently with the star;
how does He guide you and speak to you throughout your life?

DAY TWELVE

The Raising of Lazarus
John 11:28-44

When Lazarus died, Jesus was moved by the desperate cries of Lazarus' sisters. Because Mary and Martha believed in the power of Jesus, they witnessed the glory of God firsthand. This miracle not only made Lazarus new, but it also transformed Mary's and Martha's hearts as well.

Before you read, pause and clear your mind. Center yourself in God's presence and read through the scripture once. Then, choose a perspective to enter into the scene. Are you one of the characters or a silent observer? Regardless, know that this moment is full of grace.
Allow Him to make you new.

Seated on the front steps, Mary burrowed her head into her knees. Quiet sobs racked her body as friends and family members chattered softly inside the house. Her beloved brother, her best friend, was dead. Suddenly, she felt a hand resting on her shoulder. Looking up, she peered into the bloodshot eyes of her sister, Martha. Martha brushed the salty tears off Mary's cheeks gently and then whispered, "The Teacher is here and is calling for you."

Rising to her feet, Mary bounded down the path to meet Jesus. Flying over the dirt road, she rushed to Him and flung herself at his feet. Tears streamed from her eyes as she passionately cried out, "Lord, if you had been here, my brother would not have died!"

Behind Mary stood the Jews who had been inside the house. Having spotted Mary leaving the house, they had assumed she was returning to the grave and had followed to grieve with her. Upon hearing Mary's mournful words to Jesus, they, too, wept bitterly.

Moved by their tears, Jesus felt a stirring within himself. As tears began to course down his cheeks, He responded softly, "Where have you laid him?" Gathering Mary's hand tenderly in His own, He followed her a little ways down the road to Lazarus' grave.

At last, they arrived at the tomb. The cave where Lazarus's body lay was tucked into a high stone cliff. Mourners gathered around the outside of the tomb, making it difficult to walk through the crowd. Gesturing to the large stone blocking the entrance, Jesus commanded, "Take away the stone."

Martha grabbed Jesus' arm and, with desperate eyes, reminded him, "Lord, already there is a stench because he has been dead four days." Jesus stroked her cheek gently and then said to her, "Did I not tell you that if you believed, you would see the glory of God?" After biting her lip, Martha wiped her hands nervously on her linen dress and nodded at the men standing near the entrance. Together, the men strained to roll the stone away.

Once the entrance to the cave was open, Jesus gazed up to the depths of heaven and said, "Father, I thank you for having heard me. I knew that you always hear me, but I have said this for the sake of the crowd standing here, so that they may believe that you sent me."

Confused, bystanders scratched their beards and whispered to one another. Martha and Mary stood arm in arm, with the heads bent low, too terrified to look up. When Jesus had finished this prayer, he extended his arms until they were wide open. With a loud, booming voice, he ordered, "Lazarus, come out!"

Quiet gasps of dismay and disbelief rippled through the crowd, but they soon turned to cries of terror and awe as a figure began to emerge from the shadowy depths of the cave. Staggering, the once dead man walked out slowly, his hands and feet bound with thick strips of cloth. The cloth was bound so tightly around his body that it was difficult for him to move, and the rings of cloth on his face were too thick for him to speak through.

Many of the mourners turned on their heels and fled down the road as Mary and Martha clung fiercely to one another. Jesus turned to the few remaining bystanders and instructed, "Unbind him, and let him go."

HOW ARE YOU MADE NEW?

Who do you most relate to in this story?

What miracles, large or small, have you experienced?
How have they affected your life?

How do you lean on Jesus during times of sorrow?

Did I not tell you

that if you believed,

you would see the glory of God?

John 11:40

DAY THIRTEEN

The Story of Ruth and Naomi
Ruth 1:7-11,14-16,18-19

In this story, Ruth decides she will not abandon her mother-in-law, Naomi, in her time of need. Hand in hand, the women are made new as they commit the uncertainty of their lives to one another and to God's care.

Before you read, pause and clear your mind. Center yourself in God's presence and read through the scripture once. Then, choose a perspective to enter into the scene. Are you one of the characters or a silent observer? Regardless, know that this moment is full of grace.
Allow Him to make you new.

Cloaks drawn tightly across their backs, the three widows trudged wearily down the road. Rain poured from the skies, drenching every inch of their aching bodies. Their husbands had all died, leaving each woman to fend for herself. And so, their destination, and their last hope, was Judah, the land of Naomi's people.

Far from home and longing for rest, Naomi pointed to a cave near the road's edge. The three women stumbled through puddles as they made their way into the depths of the cave. Once inside, Naomi huddled together with her two daughters-in-law.

After drawing a hunk of bread out of her cloak, Naomi broke it into three meager pieces, and the women ate while the storm howled overhead. Naomi sighed heavily, the deep wrinkles on her cheeks highlighted by the small amount of light streaming in from outside. Folding her arms together resolutely, she nodded to herself as she raised her head. She had made up her mind.

Gazing upon her two daughters-in-law, she instructed them, "Go back each of you to your mother's house. May the Lord deal kindly with you, as you have dealt with the dead and with me." Drawing near, she kissed each woman tenderly on the forehead and hugged them fiercely, saying, "The Lord grant that you may find security, each of you in the house of your husband."

Seeing her resolve, the two daughters-in-law began to weep. Grasping Naomi's hands firmly, each one declared, "No, we will return with you to your people."

But Naomi said, "Turn back, my daughters, why will you go with me?" She then began to detail how little hope remained for each woman. She described the bleak and hopeless future that would await them should they choose to remain with her. With tears streaming down her face, she begged them to return to their own people.

Sobs racked the bodies of all three women as they tried to comfort one another.

Then Orpah took a deep breath, kissed her mother-in-law on both cheeks, and bade her farewell. Pulling the cloak tighter around her shoulders, she stepped out of the entrance of the cave and disappeared into the falling rain.

But Ruth clung to Naomi. Naomi urged Ruth to leave again, saying, "See, your sister-in-law has gone back to her people and to her gods; return after your sister-in-law."

Again, Ruth refused, and her voice echoed in the cave as she proclaimed, "Do not press me to leave you or to turn back from following you! Where you go, I will go."

Wrapping her arms around Naomi, Ruth looked firmly into Naomi's raw eyes as she decided, "Where you lodge, I will lodge; your people shall be my people, and your God my God. Where you die, I will die—there will I be buried."

When Naomi saw how Ruth was determined to go with her, she pressed lovingly her forehead against Ruth's and said no more. Gratitude filled Naomi's heart, and she breathed a prayer of thanksgiving. Reaching down, the two women donned their cloaks once more and continued on their journey.

HOW ARE YOU MADE NEW?

Who in this story do you most relate to? Why?

Have you ever had an experience of committing your life to another person or cause? What happened, and how were you changed because of it?

Have you ever faced a time when you were uncertain of what would happen next in your life? What happened?

Ruth's selflessness sets a powerful example. How can you be that comfort to others?

Where you go,

I will go.

Ruth 1:16

DAY FOURTEEN

The Last Supper
Luke 22:14-23

At the Last Supper, Jesus's friends thought they were sharing mere bread and wine. Unbeknownst to them, they were actually receiving the gift of Himself in the form of His most precious body and blood.

Before you read, pause and clear your mind. Center yourself in God's presence and read through the scripture once. Then, choose a perspective to enter into the scene. Are you one of the characters or a silent observer? Regardless, know that this moment is full of grace.
Allow Him to make you new.

Flickering candlelight and dancing shadows permeated the joy-filled room. After having spent all day preparing the meal, the friends smiled in relief as they reclined at the table. Some stretched their legs out and leaned their heads wearily against the backs of their wooden chairs. Others rested their elbows alongside the full platters of meat and vegetables as they gazed down the long table. With watering mouths and growling bellies, they awaited the feast eagerly as a few of the disciples finished placing bowls of fruits and nuts amongst the delicious spread.

As they all finally settled into their places, a hush came upon the room as they waited for Jesus to speak. Looking around the room, Jesus stood up from His place at the middle of the table. After raising a simple clay goblet to eye level, Jesus took a sip of wine and then let His gaze fall on each man in the room as He spoke firmly, "Take this and divide it among yourselves; for I tell you that from now on I will not drink of the fruit of the vine until the kingdom of God comes."

Surprise rippled through the disciples, who dared not speak as they watched Jesus grab a piece of crusty bread from a bowl in front of him. Straightening their backs in their seats, they watched Him gingerly tear the bread into two pieces. He took his time ripping each piece into another and another until there was enough so that each man at the table would have a piece of the loaf. Then He spoke again, "This is my body, which is given for you. Do this in remembrance of me."

As the Apostles brought the grainy bread to their lips, they marveled at Jesus' mysterious words. Slowly and deliberately, each man ate his share, and soon the sounds of friendly banter and laughter filled the room.

After everyone at the table had their fill, Jesus once again reached for His goblet of wine. He raised the cup high above His head, instantly capturing the attention of the Apostles. He looked at the cup for a moment, His eyes not looking at what He held in His hands, but rather to something far beyond the four walls of the room. The men craned their necks to see Jesus more clearly as the expression on Jesus's face was none that they had seen before.

With a steadfast voice, Jesus declared, "This cup that is poured out for you is the new covenant in my blood. But see, the one who betrays me is with me, and his hand is on the table. For the Son of Man is going as it has been determined, but woe to that one by whom he is betrayed!"

Shock washed over the disciples and several of them slammed their fists on the table in dismay. Immediately, the men began searching each other's faces with set jaws. In their own hearts, they grimly tried to determine who would do such a thing to Jesus. The candlelight flickered, casting long shadows of fear and doubt.

HOW ARE YOU MADE NEW?

How has regularly receiving the Eucharist transformed your life?

Do you believe that you are made new because of Jesus's gift of His most precious body and blood? How so?

All humans betray life in Christ's love by our sins.
What sins do you struggle with over and over again?
How can you intentionally work to rid yourself of those sins?

This is my body,

which is given for you.

Luke 22:19

DAY FIFTEEN

The Stoning of the Adulterous Woman
John 8:1-11

Just as the adulterous woman was about to be stoned to death, Jesus saved her and offered her forgiveness. Her heart was changed as she realized that she could only be made whole in His mercy.

Before you read, pause and clear your mind. Center yourself in God's presence and read through the scripture once. Then, choose a perspective to enter into the scene. Are you one of the characters or a silent observer? Regardless, know that this moment is full of grace. Allow Him to make you new.

As the sun peeked over the horizon and painted the sky with rich hues of pink and gold, Jesus walked past the towering marble columns inside the temple. After seating himself in the middle of the central chamber of the temple, Jesus began teaching the large throng of people which had followed Him.

Before long, a commotion was heard at the entrance of the temple. Angry shouting and hisses filled the air as the scribes and Pharisees entered, dragging a woman behind them. Disheveled curly hair hung down, covering much of her dirty and terror-filled face. Her wrists were bound tightly with rope, and her skirts were tattered. She wept loudly as they jerked her along.

Prodding the woman to the front of the crowd, the scribes and Pharisees forced her to stand before all of them. Scornfully, they pointed at her and said to Jesus, "Teacher, this woman was caught in the very act of adultery." The crowd began to boo louder and a few individuals made threatening gestures towards her.

Leaning towards Jesus with smug eyes and curled lips, they said, "Now in the law, Moses commanded us to stone such women. Now what do you say?" They crossed their arms and began tapping their feet, smirking slightly as they waited for His reply. Gleefully, they hoped that Jesus might answer their test incorrectly so that they could raise a charge against Him.

Jesus knelt to the ground with a furrowed brow. He stroked his beard thoughtfully, and then, after gazing at the woman's face with compassion, He began to write with His finger on the ground. Angrily, the scribes and Pharisees began to relentlessly question Him again, one after the other.

Finally, Jesus straightened up and replied, "Let anyone among you who is without sin be the first to throw a stone at her." Immediately, He bent down again and began to drag His finger lightly on the ground.

Sputtering with frustration and confusion, the Pharisees prompted and prodded Jesus, but soon they fell silent as it became clear that Jesus would not respond.

One by one, they went away, beginning with the elders, their footsteps echoing on the stone floors as they left.

Eventually, Jesus was left alone with the woman standing before him. Tears still rested in her eyes, but none fell to her cheeks. Her sobs had long ago ceased, and she stood shyly back, gazing at Jesus with an expression of wonder.

Straightening up, Jesus asked her, "Woman, where are they? Has no one condemned you?" Still in shock, the woman whispered quietly, "No one, sir." Then Jesus approached her and, loosening the bonds which fastened her wrists, He gently murmured, "Neither do I condemn you. Go on your way, and from now on do not sin again."

HOW ARE YOU MADE NEW?

What feelings surfaced as you read this story?

Did you find you related more to the adulterous woman or to the Pharisees? Why?

How has being forgiven played a transformative role in your life?
How has forgiving others changed you?

Have you ever been changed by the sacrament of Reconciliation? How so?

Go your way,

and from now on do not sin again.

John 8:11

DAY SIXTEEN

The Woman at the Well
John 4:6-15,22,25-29

At first, the Samaritan woman was hesitant. Once she gave Jesus a drink of water and conversed with Him, her eyes were opened, and she truly saw Jesus in a new light. All the while, He remained patient with her as He pursued her heart.

Before you read, pause and clear your mind. Center yourself in God's presence and read through the scripture once. Then, choose a perspective to enter into the scene. Are you one of the characters or a silent observer? Regardless, know that this moment is full of grace.
Allow Him to make you new.

Rubbing His aching back, Jesus sighed and then sat on the ground next to a well. The cool stone of the well provided the perfect resting place for Him to take a nap. Draping a hand over His eyes, Jesus prepared to take a nap while the disciples, chattering noisily, left to go into the city to buy food. As He was reclining there, the faint sound of singing filled the air.

Before long, a woman appeared with an empty clay jug on her hip and a song rising from her lips. Her long brown hair was tied up in a piece of dirty cloth, and her bare feet left tiny imprints in the dirt as she walked. At the sight of Jesus reclining near the well, she froze. Jesus drew himself upright and, looking intently at her, He begged, "Give me a drink."

Her brow wrinkled as she considered His request. Leaning

towards Him, she raised an eyebrow and asked, "How is that you, a Jew, ask a drink of me, a woman of Samaria," for she knew that Jews do not share things in common with Samaritans.

Jesus's mouth quirked and His eyes danced as He replied, "If you knew the gift of God, and who it is that is saying to you, 'Give me a drink,' you would have asked him, and he would have given you living water."

After a moment of hesitation, the woman took a step forward and set her jar down in the dust. The midday sun beat down from above as she said, "Sir, you have no bucket, and the well is deep." Crossing her arms, she tilted her head as she inquired, "Where do you get that living water? Are you greater than our ancestor Jacob, who gave us the well, and with his sons and flocks drank from it?"

Smiling gently, Jesus said to her, "Everyone who drinks of this water will be thirsty again, but those who drink of the water I will give them will never be thirsty." Gazing up towards the sky above, He added, "The water I will give will become in them a spring of water gushing up to eternal life."

The woman's eyes widened, and she dropped her mocking facade. She sat down next to Jesus. In earnest, she implored him, "Sir, give me this water that I may never be thirsty or have to keep coming here to draw water."

Then Jesus began to reveal things about the woman that she had not shared previously. In shock, she listened as he detailed her personal history. Unfolding her arms, she listened intently and then began to question him with an insatiable curiosity about the teachings of her ancestors and Jesus' own teachings.

Jesus responded with affection and patiently answered all of her questions. In charity, He told her, "You worship what you do not know; we worship what we know, for salvation is from the Jews."

After they had been sitting there for a long time, she wiped a drop of sweat off her face and stated, "I know that Messiah is coming. When he comes, he will proclaim all things to us."

And Jesus smiled gently and said to her, "I am he, the one who is speaking to you." Astonished, the woman's eyes widened. She was convinced. Just then, the disciples returned from the city carrying food in their packs. Upon seeing Jesus sitting with a woman, they drew back in surprise, but no one gasped, "What do you want?" or "Why are you speaking with her?"

Then the woman sprang to her feet, and, leaving her water jar behind, she sprinted to the city. Wildly, she raced from house to house, banging on the doors and encouraging people, saying, "Come and see a man who told me everything I have ever done!"

HOW ARE YOU MADE NEW?

Have you had an experience in which you felt Jesus slowly pursuing your heart? What happened?

How has the act of surrendering played a part of your spiritual transformation?

How do you recognize and draw closer to Christ after times of falling away?

DAY SEVENTEEN

Sarah's Prayer for Death
Tobit 3:7-17

Overwhelmed by feelings of fear, anger, and despair, Sarah called upon the name of the Lord. God heard her cries for help and restored peace to her life. Sarah learned that she lacked nothing when surrendered herself fully to the will of God.

Before you read, pause and clear your mind. Center yourself in God's presence and read through the scripture once. Then, choose a perspective to enter into the scene. Are you one of the characters or a silent observer? Regardless, know that this moment is full of grace.
Allow Him to make you new.

Tears pouring down her cheeks, Sarah knelt in the garden, her finger tips resting on her knees. The colorful flowers which danced slightly in the wind brought her no joy, for she had been married to seven husbands, but a wicked demon Asmodeus had killed each of them before they had been with her. Sarah curled up into a ball and burrowed her face in her lap as her father's maid stood behind her.

Spite dripped from the maid's narrow mouth as she pointed accusingly at Sarah and cried, "You are the one who kills your husbands! See, you have been married to seven husbands and not borne the name of a single one of them!" Crossing her arms, she slung each word insultingly, saying, "Why do you beat us? Because your husbands are dead? Go with them! May we never see a son or daughter of yours!" With that she spit at Sarah, turned on her heel, and fled the garden.

Wiping the dribble of saliva from her neck, Sarah balled up her fists and beat them against the ground. Her whole body shook violently as she heaved and then vomited from crying so hard. Gathering up her skirts, she raced up the stairs to her father's upper room. In despair, she paced back and forth across the room and plotted to hang herself.

But, after thinking it over, she decided, "Never shall they reproach my father, saying to him, 'You had only one beloved daughter but she hanged herself because of her distress.'" Rubbing her hands up and down her arms, she reasoned aloud, "I shall bring my father in his old age down in sorrow to Hades. It is better for me to not hang myself, but to pray the Lord that I may die and not listen to these reproaches anymore."

Turning towards the window, she stretched out her arms, extending them towards heaven. Then, she began to pray for death, saying, "Blessed are you, merciful God! Blessed is your name forever; let all your works praise you forever. And now, Lord, I turn my face to you, and raise my eyes toward you. Command that I be released from the earth and not listen to such reproaches anymore."

Sarah desperately pleaded her innocence to the Lord as she laid her heart bare before Him. Her fingers trembled and her breath shook as she begged him, "Already seven husbands of mine have died. Why should I still live? But if it is not pleasing to you, O Lord, to take my life, hear me in my disgrace."

At that very moment, God heard Sarah's prayers and responded with love. He sent his angel, Raphael, to heal Sarah by giving her in marriage to Tobias, son of Tobit, and by setting her free from the demon who plagued her.

HOW ARE YOU MADE NEW?

Have you had an experience of desperately calling out for God's help? What happened?

How has God restored peace to your life? When has His peace transformed you?

How can you praise God's name, even in the midst of despair, as Sarah did?

Blessed are you,

merciful God.

Tobit 3:11

DAY EIGHTEEN

The Descent of the Holy Spirit
Acts 2:1-4

When the Holy Spirit descended upon the disciples and transformed them, the unique gifts each one already possessed were brought to light. Through the work of their hands and the offering of their lives, the entire course of history was changed.

Before you read, pause and clear your mind. Center yourself in God's presence and read through the scripture once. Then, choose a perspective to enter into the scene. Are you one of the characters or a silent observer? Regardless, know that this moment is full of grace.
Allow Him to make you new.

They huddled together in the hushed room. No midday light penetrated through the cracks in the old windows for they were stuffed with shreds of faded cloth. In order to prevent anyone from entering the small space, a heavy slab of timber rested over the hastily locked doorway. A dim candle, its wax dripping down onto the weathered, wooden table, flickered from the shallow breathing of the men in the room. Fear permeated the space, filling the hearts and minds of the disciples as they murmured in hushed tones.

Suddenly, without warning, a deafening sound roared through the room. As a powerful wind extinguished the candle, a bright, fiery light burst forth in the center of the room. The men instantaneously began to shield their frightened eyes and shout to one another in terror. Wincing from the brightness of light, they scrambled against the walls and each other, certain that death was near.

As only could be choreographed by the Almighty, small tongues of fire danced forth from the bright light and settled over each disciples' head. The room was now lit, not by one lonely candle, but by the Spirit pouring forth over each individual. Curiously, the disciples gazed at each other, the corners of their mouths slowly turning to wide smiles of joy. Their souls began to dance in the same glorious movement as the flames above them.

One of disciples opened his mouth to speak, but the jubilant statement that spilled from his lips was in the language of a distant land. Another disciple responded in surprise, but he also spoke in words previously unknown to them. Then each began to speak different languages, filled with awe at the knowledge that though the words were of an unfamiliar dialect, they could understand each other completely. Their elation tumbled forth as they laughed and hugged one another, crying out, "He is here!"

HOW ARE YOU MADE NEW?

Where did you place yourself in this story? Why?

Has the Holy Spirit played a significant part of your life?
Why or why not?

What God-given gifts are you called to share with the world?
When has the surrendering of these talents made you new?

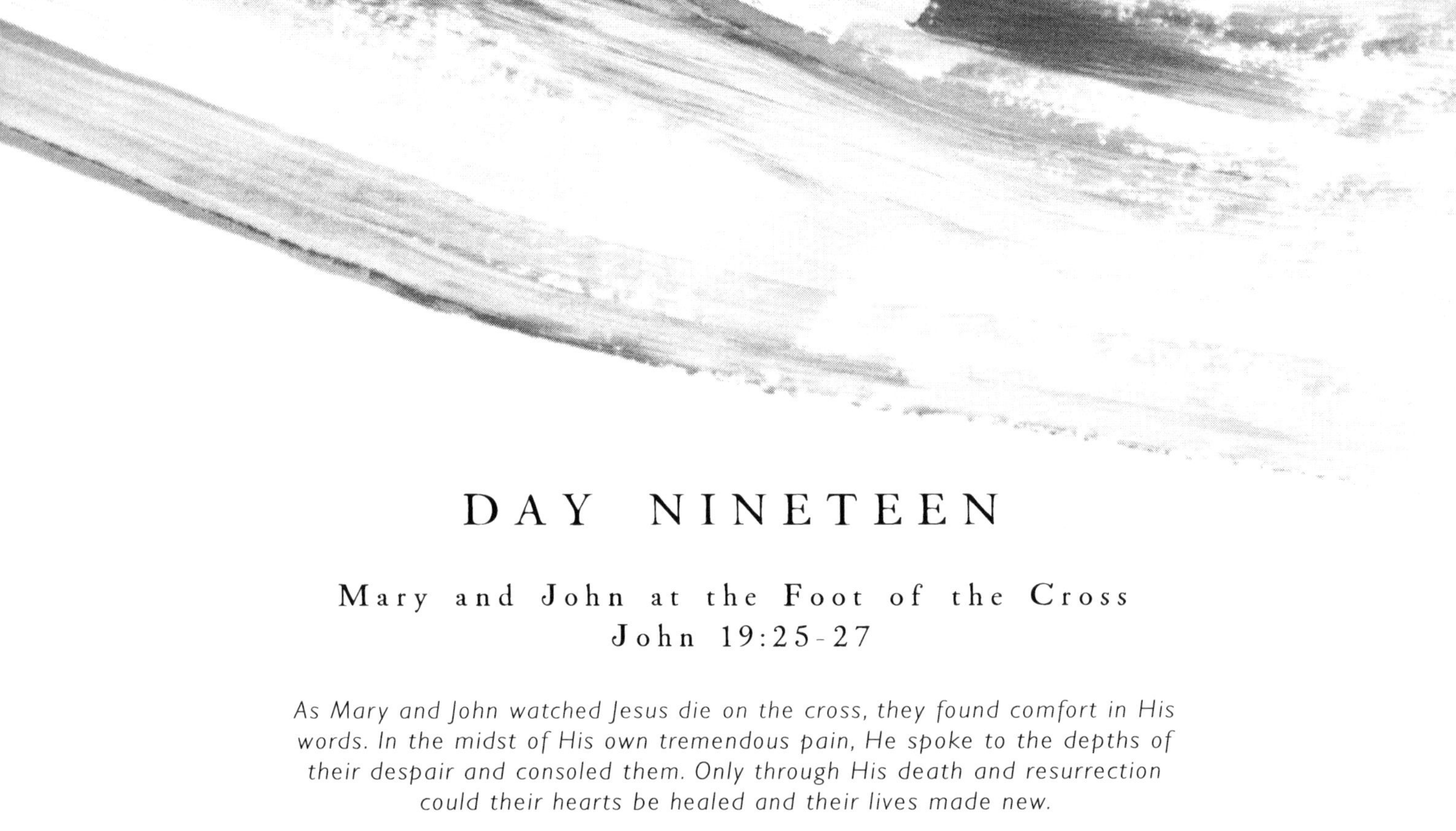

DAY NINETEEN

Mary and John at the Foot of the Cross
John 19:25-27

As Mary and John watched Jesus die on the cross, they found comfort in His words. In the midst of His own tremendous pain, He spoke to the depths of their despair and consoled them. Only through His death and resurrection could their hearts be healed and their lives made new.

*Before you read, pause and clear your mind. Center yourself in God's presence and read through the scripture once. Then, choose a perspective to enter into the scene. Are you one of the characters or a silent observer? Regardless, know that this moment is full of grace.
Allow Him to make you new.*

Mary wearily pulled her woven shawl tighter around her sunken shoulders. Exhausted, she slumped on the hard dirt ground at Golgotha's crest. The warm midday wind relentlessly blew dust all around her, and as she wiped her tear stained face, streaks of mud were left behind on her weathered cheeks.

Her gentle eyes were raw and bloodshot from the tears she had shed all day. Her mind kept replaying the events of the morning. Mary wept softly as she recalled her precious child being brutally scourged, crowned with thick thorns, and forced to carry the heavy wood upon which He would soon die. And yet, here she knelt at the foot of the cross, her gaze never wavering from her Son and His limp, bloodied body hanging above her. Her heart had been pierced to the core, but in the depths of her love, she remained steadfast in her devotion to Him until the end. He would always be her Son.

Behind Mary stood her sister, Mary, and Mary Magdalene. Every so often she would hear their quiet weeping as they rested their hands on her shoulders. Jesus's dearest friend, John, stood solemnly beside her. Through tear-filled eyes, John viewed with horror the somber scene before him. He refused to succumb to the waves of grief passing through his body. He would not waver in his resolve to be strong and remain close to the woman who had born Jesus into the world. She needed him in this dreadful nightmare. And deep down inside, John knew that he needed her, too.

Slowly, with every ounce of strength that He had, Jesus lifted His head and looked directly at Mary and John. Blood dripped down His sweating, swollen face and His lips were dry and cracked. His breathing was labored. The weight of His own body was slowly killing Him.

As His once strong lungs now denied Him the power of breath, Jesus managed to utter, "Woman, here is your son." A pause and then, with another spurt of labor, "Here is your mother." Jesus strenuously exhaled from the exhaustion of His own speech as Love poured forth from Him into the hearts of Mary and John.

Upon hearing these words, John let out a loud sob, collapsing next to Mary. He wrapped his strong arms around her trembling body and felt the weight of her own grief sinking into his. Heartbroken and yet made new, he promised to always care for Mary in his own home.

HOW ARE YOU MADE NEW?

Have you had an experience of deep consolation in the Lord? What happened?

How have you been made new by an experience of grief or loss?

How can you show the kind of love Mary did, despite trials, in your day-to-day life?

Woman, here is your son.

John 19:26

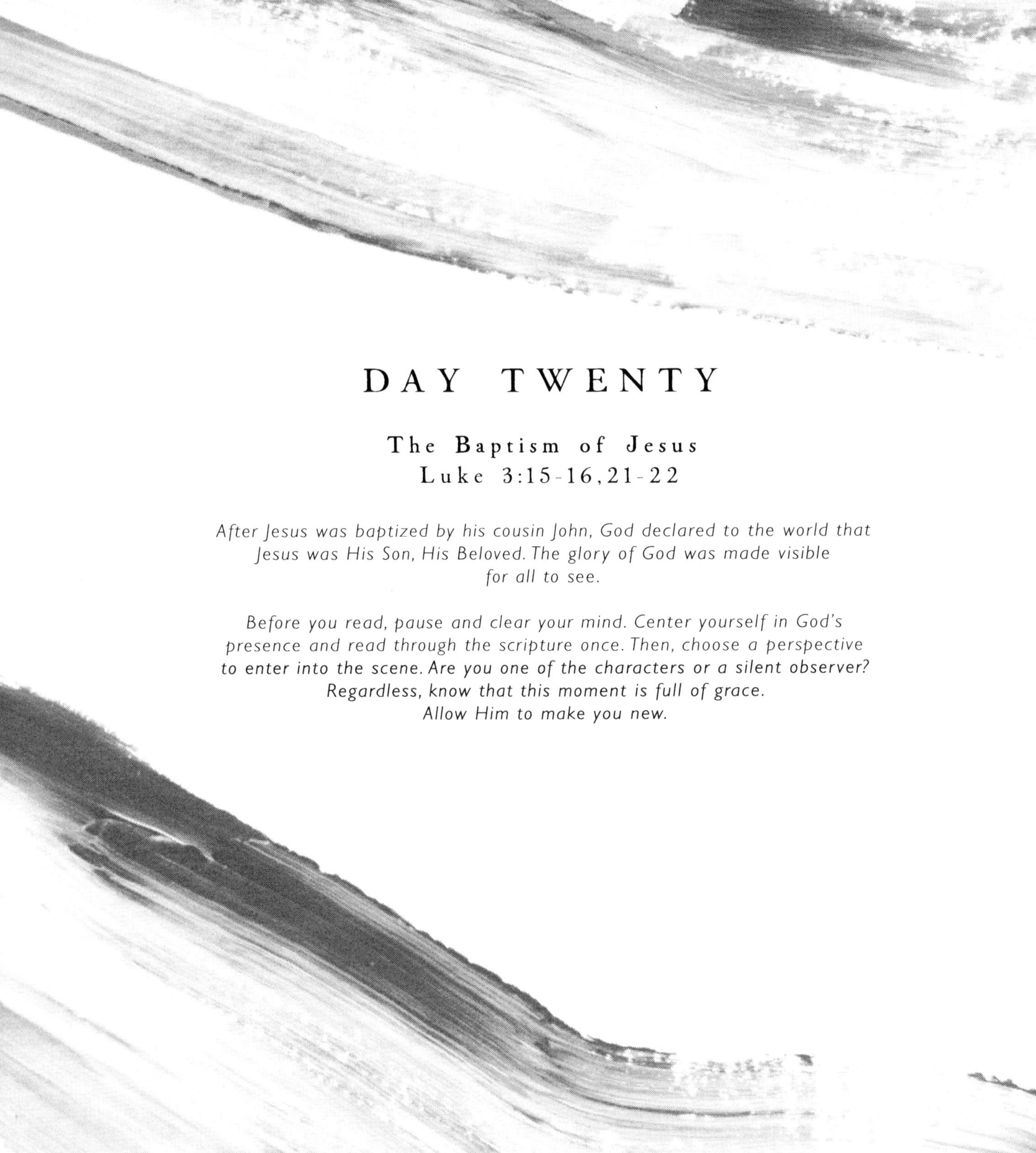

DAY TWENTY

The Baptism of Jesus
Luke 3:15-16,21-22

After Jesus was baptized by his cousin John, God declared to the world that Jesus was His Son, His Beloved. The glory of God was made visible for all to see.

Before you read, pause and clear your mind. Center yourself in God's presence and read through the scripture once. Then, choose a perspective to enter into the scene. Are you one of the characters or a silent observer? Regardless, know that this moment is full of grace. Allow Him to make you new.

Whispers spread throughout the crowd as everyone craned their necks and hoped to catch a glimpse of John. *Could this be the one for whom we have all waited? Could this John be our Messiah?*

Turning around, John caught sight of the gaggle of people behind him. Shaking his head slightly, he sighed exasperatedly. He clambered up onto a nearby rock and stood on it. As he extended his hands, the crowd fell silent, eager to hear whatever he had to say.

John scratched his beard and pursed his lips as he gazed over the crowd. Then, taking a deep breath, he answered them in a thunderous but kind voice, "I baptize with water; but the one who is more powerful than I is coming." Pointing to the heavens, he declared, "I am not worthy to untie the thong of his sandals."

The whispers grew louder as the crowd pondered the meaning of his words. Leaping off the rock, John plodded through the muck and entered the cool water.

Now, when all of the people were baptized, John ran his fingers through his thick hair and started making his way back to the shore. Just then, a movement near the water's edge caught his eye. A man appeared, clothed in a simple tunic. John broke into a wide smile; it was Jesus.

Jesus waded through the water to greet John, causing ripples to spread out across the surface of the river. As Jesus approached, John began to kneel in the river, but Jesus lifted him to his feet. Together, the two men conversed in hushed tones. Then, John reached into the the depths of the sparkling water. The cool water spilled from John's hands over Jesus' upturned face, streaming over His closed eyes and down His chest and back. When John was finished baptizing Jesus, Jesus bent his head and prayed fervently as the people crowding the banks of the river watched intently.

Suddenly, the whole earth rumbled and a ray of light shot forth from the heavens as the sky appeared to split in two. Bystanders screamed in panic and dived behind rocks, trembling from head to toe. The Holy Spirit descended from the heavens before coming to rest lightly upon Jesus in the form of a dove. Then, a booming voice echoed forth, vibrating the whole of the valley. The voice from heaven proclaimed, "You are my Son, the Beloved; with you I am well pleased."

HOW ARE YOU MADE NEW?

Do you believe that you, too, are God's beloved child? Why or why not?

How does this knowledge change your heart for the Lord and determine how you live your life?

When has Christ renewed you and helped you grow?

You are my Son, the Beloved;
with you I am well pleased.
Luke 3:22

Allow Him

to make you new.

CONNECT

www.livetodaywellco.com
Instagram @livetodaywellco
facebook.com/livetodaywellco
#livetodaywellco

Made in the USA
San Bernardino, CA
06 January 2019